DRUGS
AND
YOU

Arnold Madison

JULIAN MESSNER

Published by Julian Messner, a division of
Silver Burdett Press, Inc., Simon & Schuster, Inc.,
Prentice Hall Bldg., Englewood Cliffs, NJ 07632.
Revised Edition, 1990
JULIAN MESSNER and colophon are trademarks of
Simon & Schuster, Inc. Design by Iris Weinstein
Manufactured in the United States of America.

Library of Congress Cataloging-in-Publication Data
Madison, Arnold.
Drugs and you / Arnold Madison.
p. cm.
Summary: Discusses the major drugs in use today, their
history, their effect on the mind and body, their harmful
and beneficial uses, and the control of illegal drug traffic.
ISBN 0-671-69147-3   ISBN 0-671-69148-1 (pbk.)
1. Drug abuse—Juvenile literature. 2. Drugs—Juvenile
literature. [1. Drug abuse. 2. Drugs.] I. Title
HV5801.M25 1990
613.8—dc20   89-27788
CIP
AC

Lib. ed. 10 9 8 7 6 5 4 3 2 1
Paper ed. 10 9 8 7 6 5 4 3 2 1

For Kathy Kane, who gave me a helping hand

Acknowledgments

The author wishes to express his appreciation to the following people for their assistance in the preparation of *Drugs and You*: Robert L. Bernstein, D.D.S.; Mrs. Rosemarie Gaudioso, elementary school teacher, Plainedge Public Schools, N.Y.; Mrs. Ethel Kramer, elementary school teacher, Farmingdale Public Schools, N.Y.; Commissioner Francis L. Looney, Nassau County (N.Y.) Police Department; the Los Angeles County Sheriff's Department; Lawrence F. Nazarian, M.D.; Mr. Roy Schoenberg, Principal, John H. West Elementary School, Bethpage, N.Y.; Robert I. Tugendhaft, M.D.; and Dr. Jane A. Slezak.

CONTENTS

DRUGS
AND
YOU

1

The Drug List

Recently a teacher in a Midwestern elementary school startled her twenty-three students by asking them these three questions:

1. Do you know what drugs are?
2. Do you know anyone who uses drugs?
3. Do you use drugs?

She told the class to write their answers, but not their names, on the sheets of paper she had given them. After the answers were collected and counted, she announced the results.

"Question number one: twenty-three yeses. Question number two: fourteen yeses and nine noes."

Heads turned in all directions as the students wondered who had answered yes and who had answered no.

The teacher continued. "…And question number three: twenty-two noes and one maybe."

Heads turned again and there were whispers. But "maybe" didn't give him- or herself away.

"Everyone answered yes to the first question," the teacher went on, "so I suggest we begin by making a list of drugs on the chalkboard. Name all the drugs you know and I'll write them down."

The students quickly named marijuana, heroin, and cocaine. Then they added crack and speed. Then they stopped.

A girl at the back of the room spoke up. "Sleeping pills and diet pills," she said. "They're drugs, I'm sure. My father had to take sleeping pills when he came back from the hospital."

"Aren't steroids drugs?" a boy asked.

"They certainly are," the teacher told him. "Many high-school athletes as well as professional sports people risk serious illness and death by taking steroids to build up their bodies."

"I know someone who uses drugs," said a boy in front. "My dad. He uses them all the time." Everyone stared at him. "It's a drug called novocaine," he continued. "My dad's a dentist and he gives it to his patients to stop them from feeling the pain when he's fixing their teeth."

"That's right," said the teacher, grinning. "But it's really your father's patients who take that drug, not him. When I spoke about using drugs, I meant the people who actually take them."

Another student asked, "What about a flu shot? Isn't that like a drug? I'm not sure, but I know I've had them."

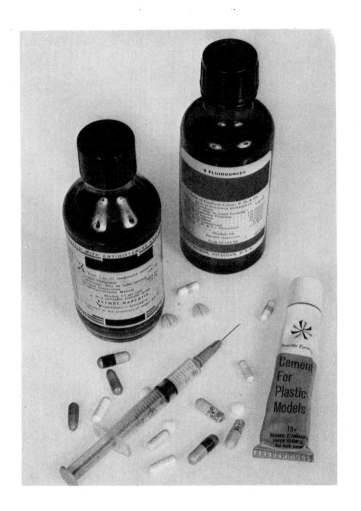

Cough medicine, vitamins, diet pills, sleeping pills, aspirin, penicillin, and also model-airplane glue were some of the drugs that the class named in answer to their teacher's questions about drugs.

"A flu shot certainly is a drug," said the teacher. "Doctors use it to prevent people from getting the flu."

Now the room was buzzing. Hands went up one after another. The students realized that too often they used the word *drugs* to mean only dangerous drugs. But medicines are also drugs. So they named the various kinds of medicine

3

With drugs and drug use as their subject, fourth graders in Winchester, Virginia, collected newspaper and magazine articles, read books, and made posters that showed what drugs are, how they are used, and by whom. Then they wrote reports and talked about drugs in library and classroom discussion groups.

their doctors had told them to take. Then they started naming simple medicines that anyone can buy at the drugstore, such as aspirin, cough syrup, and vitamin pills.

A few minutes later they had to stop, for there was no more room on the chalkboard. After studying the board, the dentist's son summed everything up neatly.

"That's mostly a list of things we didn't think were drugs," he said. "If the only drugs were cocaine and those other ones we named first, a drugstore wouldn't be a drugstore, would it?"

Then the student who had asked about flu shots said, "Can I change my answer to question three now? I'd like to say yes instead of maybe."

Twenty-two other hands flashed into the air as others wanted to change their answers. The teacher decided the best thing to do was to let everyone answer the three questions all over again.

It was very easy for her to announce the results this time. "Class," she said, "on questions one, two, and three we have a total of sixty-nine yeses."

Everyone, including the teacher, was smiling. Now they really were beginning to understand what drugs are.

2

Basic Facts about Drugs

Knowing the names of different drugs is a useful start in learning about drugs. But it is only a start. There is so much more we need to know.

What Are Drugs?

Drugs are chemical substances that can cause changes in our bodies.

Does your mother or father give you aspirin when you have a headache? The aspirin causes several changes in your body. It helps to get rid of the aches and pains in your muscles as well as stopping your headache.

Does your doctor give you an antibiotic when you have a serious infection? Antibiotics are powerful drugs that kill germs that have invaded your body.

Almost all the pills and liquid medicines in this medicine chest have one thing in common: they are drugs, and they cause chemical changes in the body.

Aspirin and antibiotics are drugs. So are novocaine, nose drops, cough syrup, heroin, crack, and marijuana. In fact, there are thousands and thousands of different drugs, far too many to list in this book.

All these drugs have one thing in common: they are chemical substances that can cause changes in the human body.

Are the Foods We Eat Drugs? Not every substance that can cause changes in our bodies is a drug. For example, foods can make us fat or thin, help us stay healthy, or even make us sick. They cause changes in our bodies, but they are not drugs.

Drugs differ from foods in three important ways. First, all drugs are chemical substances, but only some foods have chemicals in them. Second, drugs can cause many more changes in us than foods can. For example, antibiotics cure many diseases, but potatoes do not cure any. Third, many healthy people can go without drugs for weeks, months, or even years, but they cannot go without food for more than a few days.

How Do We Take Drugs?

We take most drugs by swallowing them. The drugs we swallow are either pills or capsules, such as aspirin or antibiotics, or liquids, such as cough syrup.

We take some drugs by injection. The nurse or doctor uses a thin, hollow needle to inject liquid drugs into the body. Injecting is the fastest way to make drugs produce changes inside us.

A third way to take drugs is by breathing them in, or inhaling them. Some surgeons put their patients to sleep

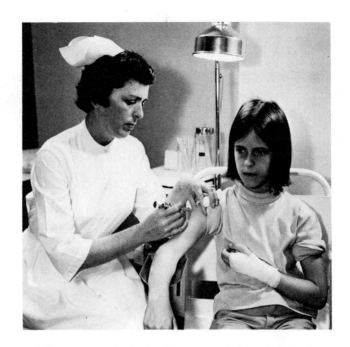

The nurse is injecting some serum into the girl's arm. This serum will prevent her from getting tetanus, which can be fatal. Injection is only one way of taking drugs, but it is the fastest way to get the drug to work in the body.

before an operation by having them breathe in a drug in the form of a gas. And cigarette smokers inhale a drug called nicotine every time they inhale cigarette smoke.

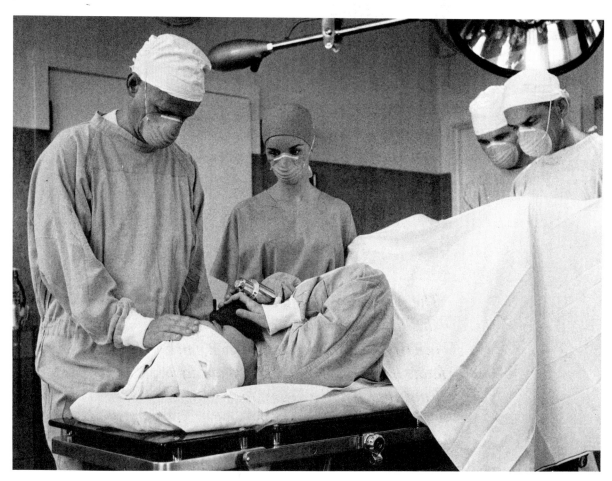

Another way to take drugs is to breathe them in. To ease the patient's pain during a surgical operation, he or she may be given an anesthetic in the form of a gas.

Whatever ways drugs are taken, they eventually get into the bloodstream, which carries them around the body.

How Can Drugs Change Us?

The changes caused by drugs are called drug effects. It is important to remember that one drug can often have several different effects. Some drug users experience effects they did not expect. This can frighten them and may harm their bodies.

Drugs can save us from death by curing illnesses. They can just as easily, and even more quickly, kill us. Drugs can do many other things, too. They can help keep us healthy or make us ill, take away our appetite or make us very hungry, wake us up or put us to sleep, make us feel happy or make us feel sad. Drugs can drive normal people mad or help cure people who are mentally ill.

How Do Drugs Actually Affect the Body?

Some years ago, a doctor treated three young boys who were very ill with scarlet fever. He gave each of them exactly the same amount of penicillin. All three boys soon got well, but not before one had vomited a lot and another had broken out in a widespread rash.

Penicillin not only cured the boys' scarlet fever, but it also caused other effects, which are called side effects. Side effects do not happen to everyone. Nor are they caused by every drug. However, the side effects caused in the two boys with scarlet fever can be avoided by using new drugs that can cure as well as penicillin but do not produce such side effects.

But why do side effects happen? Because the chemistry of the human body is very complicated. The body makes and uses its own natural chemicals. These chemicals control food digestion, the flow of the blood, muscle and bone growth, and many other bodily activities. So the effects of a drug depend on what happens when the drug, a chemical substance, is added to the body's own chemicals.

The body chemistry of one person is never exactly the same as any other person's. That is why the *same* drug can sometimes produce different effects in different people.

Are Drugs the Same as Medicines?

A medicine is any substance used to cure, control, or prevent illness or pain. If a drug is used for that purpose, it is a medicine. Cough syrup used as directed to stop a cough is a medicine. But cough syrup is *not* a medicine when it is drunk by someone just because it tastes good or because large amounts produce a "high." If a drug is used for some other, nonmedical purpose, it is no longer a medicine.

The question of whether or not a drug is a medicine doesn't usually depend on what it is. It depends on how the drug is *used.*

3

The Use and Misuse of Medicinal Drugs

Take one tablet a day." "Use one or two drops in each nostril, two to four times a day." "Take one tablespoonful every four hours." "Dissolve one tablet in water and drink."

Do these directions sound familiar to you? They probably do because they are the directions you will find on containers of vitamins, nose drops, cough syrups, and antacid tablets (for settling upset stomachs).

The purpose of the directions is to make sure that we use the drugs properly and safely. That is why there are federal laws about the directions that must appear on drug-container labels.

Follow the Directions!

The label on a drug container must tell us the name of the drug and what the drug should be used for. For example,

14

The label on a drug container has important information. It tells how much of the drug you should use and how often you should take it.

an aspirin-bottle label says "Aspirin" and tells us that it is "For the relief of pain due to headache, neuralgia, and muscular aches."

The label also tells us the dosage, or amount to take, and how often we should take it. Many drugs have different doses for children and for adults. Most nonprescription-drug labels also tell the maximum amount that can be safely taken in a single day.

Other directions on the label may warn us about side effects that may occur when we take the drug. Cold pills, for instance, make some people sleepy. Side effects can be much worse for people with certain illnesses. So the label may warn people with heart disease or high blood pressure not to take the drug without first consulting their doctor.

Using a drug properly and safely depends on following

the directions on the label. It can also depend on following the advice of the doctor. In fact, many drugs should be taken *only* when the doctor says so.

Prescription and Nonprescription Drugs

What would happen if you walked into a drugstore and asked for some aspirin and a powerful antibiotic drug? The druggist would sell you the aspirin. But he or she would not sell you the antibiotic unless you had a prescription for it from a doctor. Strong antibiotics are prescription drugs.

A prescription is a doctor's written permission for you to have the drug, as well as his or her instructions to the druggist. The druggist prepares the prescription drug according to these instructions and writes directions on the label so you can follow the doctor's orders.

Using prescriptions is one way in which doctors and druggists try to make sure that powerful drugs are not misused. They want to be sure that the right patient takes the correct amount of the prescribed drug.

Aspirin can be bought without a prescription. So can vitamins, cough medicines, and many other drugs. The nonprescription drugs, or over-the-counter drugs, are not as powerful as the prescription ones. But that does not

The doctor has examined his patient to find out what is wrong with him. Now he is writing a prescription for the patient to have filled by the druggist. A prescription tells the name of the drug, the amount to be prepared by the druggist, and how often the patient should take it. The druggist will type this information on the drug-container label. He or she will also include the names of the patient and the doctor, and the date the prescription was filled.

mean that they are always safer to take. All drugs, prescription and nonprescription, are safe to take *only* when they are used properly.

How People Misuse Medicinal Drugs

People misuse medicinal drugs mainly in two ways. One, they don't follow the directions on the label of the drug container. Two, they don't get their doctor's advice, or else they ignore the advice after they get it.

Some people are just careless about the directions on labels. They don't bother to make sure they are taking the right dose at the right time. They forget about—or don't even read—warnings about side effects. They may even get their drugs mixed up, so they are not taking the right drug.

Other people deliberately do not follow the directions on drug labels. For example, there are people who believe that if a small amount of aspirin gets rid of a slight headache, then a lot of aspirin cures a very bad headache. They find out how wrong they are when taking too much aspirin makes them sick.

Some people don't bother with advice from doctors. Instead, they decide for themselves what illnesses they have and what drugs they should take. They may know enough about medicine to know which drug to take for which illness. But, because they are not doctors, they are often wrong about which illness they really have.

What Happens When People Misuse Drugs?

When they are used as directed, drugs are helpful and usually safe. When *not* used as directed, the same medications can be dangerous, because they can easily upset the chemical balance of the body. Remember, the body's chemistry is tricky and delicate. Body chemicals do many important jobs that keep you alive. If your body needs help, it will give you warning signals: the symptoms of illness. Then you can go to your doctor, who will know what drug will help you.

It can be just as dangerous to misuse over-the-counter drugs as to misuse prescription drugs. For instance, thousands of people get sick every year because they misuse one very common over-the-counter medication: aspirin.

Many people have lived to regret misusing drugs, that is, taking the wrong dose or the wrong drug, which made them very sick. But many other people have not lived to regret it—the misuse of drugs has killed them.

19

4

Drug Misuse
and the Law

The misuse of drugs can harm a person's health. But it can be dangerous in another way as well. Anyone who misuses a drug may also be breaking the law.

If you listen to radio or television news programs or read newspapers, you know that many people are arrested for selling, owning, or using various drugs.

Some of the drugs involved in these arrests are legal prescription drugs that have been sold or used illegally. It is within the law, for example, for someone to take sleeping pills as long as he or she has orders from a doctor to do so. Sleeping pills are a legal prescription drug. But if a person takes them without a doctor's permission, he or she is breaking the law—that is, using a legal drug illegally.

If the druggist sold that person the sleeping pills without asking for a prescription, the druggist is breaking the law. If a friend or stranger sold the drug to the misuser, that person is breaking the law.

But most drugs involved in police arrests are *illegal* drugs. Some of them are cocaine, crack, and heroin.

Why People Misuse Drugs

What makes people misuse drugs? They may begin misusing medicinal drugs because they want to treat their own illnesses. But some people misuse illegal drugs. The typical young drug misuser begins taking these drugs for any or all of the following reasons:
- He or she may become very curious about drugs after listening to friends who take drugs. The person hears

Newspapers often have articles about drug misuse and the law. Although they keep you informed, as do television, radio, and maga- zines, it is also good to use books, classroom lectures, and advice from qualified experts to increase your knowledge of this subject.

them say, "It's fun!" "It's cool!" "Fantastic!" So, he or she decides to find out whether they're right.

- The same friends may urge the person to join them in misusing some drug. They may even threaten to leave him or her out of all their activities if the person does not join them. So, someone may start taking drugs because he or she does not want to lose friends.
- People may begin to believe that they can solve or forget their problems by taking drugs. A person may be having trouble at home or in school, then turn to drugs in the hope that they will make the problems go away.
- Some people think that because their parents and other adults are *against* misusing drugs, young people should be *for* it. They want to rebel against authority.
- Others may hear about so many other people who misuse drugs that they say to themselves, "Why shouldn't I?" They think it is okay to go along with the crowd, even though they may know nothing about drugs and what they can do to people.

Illegal Drugs and the Law

There are many different federal and state laws about illegal drugs. Depending on which law and which drug are involved, it can be illegal to make, own, sell, or take an

People who are arrested for using or selling illegal drugs often find that they have hurt their friends and family as well as themselves.

illegal drug. According to some laws, a person can be arrested for just being in the same room or car with someone else who has an illegal drug in his or her pocket!

If a person is found guilty of breaking a drug law, he or she may be sent to jail. If very young, the person may be

23

sent to live in a youth center. After serving the sentence, he or she will meet with the same difficulties that face people who have been in jail for other crimes. For instance, can this person find a job? Can he or she go back to school? Will family and friends accept the convicted criminal?

Many people, especially those who are young, think that the drug laws are bad laws and that they should be changed. But whether they are good or bad doesn't change the fact that they are laws. In our society, people who break the law are punished. A well-known lawyer recently said, "Those of us who are aware of the problem are doing all we can to change what we consider to be bad laws; but unless and until they are changed, they are the law of the land and will be enforced by the police and the courts."

5

Drug Abuse and
Drug Addiction

The serious misuse of drugs for a long period of time is called drug abuse. A drug abuser does not just misuse drugs now and again. He or she misuses them day after day.

To a drug abuser, drugs are part of everyday life. The person is used to taking them and does not think he or she can get along without them. For that individual, taking drugs is a habit—a necessary habit.

Drug Habituation

Do you usually chew gum on the way to school, take the same seat every evening at the dinner table, or tap your pencil against your teeth while you study? All of these activities are habits. Everyone has habits. They are part of our everyday lives.

Like other people, a drug abuser has many habits. But the most important one for that person is taking drugs. That individual may be willing to give up most other habits—even that of eating regularly—just to keep the drug-taking habit.

The drug abuser is convinced *in the mind* that he or she wants or needs drugs. Scientists call this condition drug habituation, or psychological dependence.

Drug Addiction

What happens when you miss a meal or even several meals in a row? You feel very hungry. You may have aches and pains in your stomach, head, and muscles. All you can think about is food.

The reason you feel this way is because your body needs food every day. Your body is so used to getting food that you can become ill if you miss meals.

Some drug abusers get very sick if they stop taking drugs. This is because their bodies—not just their minds—get used to the drugs. Their bodies *need* the drugs as much as your body needs food.

What happens is that certain drugs gradually change the chemistry of the abuser's body. The body becomes so used to getting the drug that it depends on receiving it.

When someone becomes used to a drug, his system cannot do without it. The drug changes his body chemistry. Because he does not eat properly or take care of himself, he is likely to become sick. He may lose interest in everything except getting his next dose of the drug.

Also, the drug abuser's body chemistry changes in such a way that the effect of the drug becomes weaker and weaker. The abuser has to take the drug more often and in larger amounts to keep getting the original effect. His or her body gets used to and can tolerate, or put up with, more and more of the drug. This condition is called tolerance.

When a drug abuser in this condition suddenly stops taking drugs, sickness occurs. The body became used to the drug gradually, but now it suddenly has to get used to not having the drug. The more tolerance that has built up in the body, the sicker the abuser gets when he or she stops using the drug. This sickness, called withdrawal sickness, can be so bad that it can kill a drug abuser.

A drug abuser who has built up tolerance and suffers from withdrawal sickness is a drug addict. The person suffers from drug addiction, or physical dependence.

Is Every Drug Abuser a Drug Addict?

Only certain drugs cause addiction. These drugs are called addictive drugs and include heroin and morphine. A drug abuser who takes these drugs regularly usually becomes a drug addict.

But a drug abuser who smokes marijuana, for example, will not become an addict, because marijuana is a nonaddictive drug. Most drugs are nonaddictive.

So not all drug abusers suffer from drug addiction. But *all* drug abusers do suffer from drug habituation. And in some ways, which we will explore later in this book, drug habituation is just as serious a problem as drug addiction.

6

Alcohol, Caffeine, and Nicotine

You have probably seen many television programs and movies in which a business executive gets up in the morning, has a cup of coffee, and rushes to his or her office. There, while hard at work, the person smokes numerous cigarettes. In the evening the individual returns home, where he or she has a drink of liquor before dinner.

There is nothing unusual about this scene because it happens all the time in everyday life. Millions of Americans drink liquor and coffee and smoke cigarettes. But many of them never realize that they are actually using drugs.

The alcohol in liquor is a drug. So are the caffeine in coffee and the nicotine in cigarettes. These drugs are three of the ones most often used, misused, and abused by Americans.

Many adults like to drink and smoke. However, few of them seem to realize that they are feeling the effects of two powerful drugs—alcohol and nicotine.

Alcohol

Alcohol is the common name for a chemical substance called ethyl alcohol. Most people take the drug by drinking whiskey, gin, wine, or beer. Alcohol is a legal drug. Adults

31

can buy it without a prescription in most parts of the United States. Children, however, are not allowed to purchase or use alcohol.

Alcohol affects the brain, especially the part of the brain that controls the way a person behaves. However, a person's behavior under the influence of alcohol depends on why the individual drinks and how much he or she drinks, as well as on the drinker's own personality.

Many adults drink alcohol when they get together with friends or relatives. They don't drink a lot. They may get slightly "high," but they rarely or never get drunk. They drink for various reasons, but the most common ones are that alcohol helps them relax and stop worrying. It makes them feel less shy and nervous when they are with other people, and it makes them feel more cheerful.

But some people drink much more alcohol and do it very often. These people misuse and abuse alcohol.

Alcohol is an addictive drug. Addiction to alcohol is called alcoholism, and the addict is called an alcoholic. Like other addicts, the alcoholic builds up tolerance to the drug. He or she soon needs more and more of it in order to keep getting the same effect. If the alcoholic suddenly stops taking the drug, he or she suffers from withdrawal sickness.

There is no one reason why people become alcoholics. Most alcoholics are people who have difficulty facing the problems in their lives. So they "drown" their troubles in drink. But drinking itself usually becomes a problem—often the biggest problem in their lives.

Large doses of alcohol can damage the liver, brain, and stomach. Alcohol also interferes with the digestion of food, and as a result alcoholics suffer from poor health. Alcoholics have been known to choke to death in their sleep. This happens because too much alcohol causes the person to become unconscious. If the person vomits while lying down, the vomited material may be swallowed and inhaled into the lungs. The air supply is cut off, and the person suffocates.

Alcoholics often have a hard time holding or finding jobs. Family and friends may leave them. And, because alcohol affects a person's judgment, many alcoholics drive when they are drunk. About half of all the people killed in traffic accidents each year die because either they or other people were driving while drunk. As a result, states are passing tougher laws that fine drunken drivers or even sentence them to jail.

There have been other legal attempts to limit drinking. Today, it is illegal in all fifty states to buy alcohol if you are under the age of twenty-one.

What has happened now that these tougher driving and purchase laws have been passed? First, there has been a slight drop in the number of deaths due to drunk driving. But these laws have created other serious problems.

Many college leaders feel there is now *more* drunk driving among their students than there used to be. At one time, young people could drink legally on some college campuses. Now, in order to drink, they must leave their school areas, usually in cars.

Parties in deserted places have also increased among high-school students. As a result crime has increased. With no adults supervising the parties, there are fights, robberies, and even murders at underage drinking parties.

To fight this problem, young people are forming groups throughout the United States. High schoolers are joining Students Against Drunk Driving (SADD). SADD members speak to people their own age. They help them to limit their drinking. Some SADD members will drive drunk teenagers home from parties. They have also set up the assigned-driver program. If several teenagers intend to drink, one person in the group agrees to be the assigned driver and promises not to drink. That person is responsible for driving the others home.

Most communities see that groups like SADD are doing a better job of preventing trouble than could be done by passing harsher laws against drunken drivers or by raising the drinking age. The reason is that young people are helping young people. This often works better than laws passed by adults.

Recently, an expert on drugs was speaking to a group of

elementary-school students. One youngster asked, "What is the worst drug?"

The answer? "Alcohol," the expert replied. "Not only because it can have such a bad effect on the body, but because many people never even think of it as a drug. I've heard parents say that they were glad their teenagers were getting drunk every weekend rather than smoking pot. It would be best if the teenagers did neither. But I would be much more frightened by abuse of alcohol."

In fact, alcoholism is the most serious drug problem in the United States. At one time, many teenagers first experimented with alcohol between the ages of fifteen and seventeen. Today, some people are even younger when they start to drink.

There are ten million known alcoholics in the United States, but government officials estimate that there could be as many as thirty million Americans who are addicted to alcohol. And the damage that results from alcoholism is great. Every year there are many diseases, broken families, financial disasters, and deaths caused by alcoholism.

Caffeine

Did you have a cola drink today? Or a cup of hot cocoa? If you did, you probably had a small amount of caffeine.

Caffeine is a drug found in coffee, tea, cola, and cocoa. Almost all Americans use at least one of these drinks. And there is no legal reason why they should not.

Most people take caffeine because they believe it makes them feel more alert, less tired and sleepy. That is why so many people start the day with a cup of coffee. Drivers traveling long distances and students studying late at night often drink large quantities of coffee so they won't fall asleep. Or they may buy caffeine pills at the drugstore and take those instead of drinking lots of coffee.

But caffeine is often misused and abused. When people take in too much of it, they become restless and irritable. They often have trouble thinking clearly. And they find it hard to get to sleep. For these reasons, some people prefer to drink the special kinds of coffee and soft drinks that do not contain caffeine.

Caffeine abuse is not as dangerous as alcoholism, because it does not cause serious illness or death. Although abusers do suffer from the effects of habituation, caffeine is not addictive.

Nicotine

"Warning: The Surgeon General Has Determined That Cigarette Smoking is Dangerous to Your Health." By law, these words or other warnings must appear on all American cigarette packages. The reason for the warning is that cigarette smoke contains several drugs, especially nicotine, which is a powerful chemical substance. Scientists and doctors have found that nicotine either causes or helps to cause many illnesses.

Nevertheless, millions of Americans continue to smoke. Why? The main reason is that they cannot break their addiction to nicotine. In 1988 the Surgeon General of the United States declared nicotine as addictive as heroin.

Some cigarette smokers claim that smoking helps to calm their nerves. Actually, nicotine is a mild stimulant that speeds up rather than slowing down or calming the activity of the brain.

Many young people start smoking because they think it makes them look grown-up. But more and more of them realize that smoking cigarettes is dangerous. Nicotine is actually a poison. Large amounts of it can make people feel sick and dizzy, blur their eyesight, and give them headaches and diarrhea. They also know that long-time cigarette smokers can get such serious illnesses as emphysema, heart disease, and lung cancer.

Cigarettes are a legal drug for adults. Although they are illegal for children, the law is often broken. But many people, young and old, believe that nicotine is so dangerous that cigarettes should be made illegal for everyone.

7

Heroin and
Other Narcotics

Narcotics are various drugs that all produce similar effects. A person under the influence of a strong narcotic feels sleepy or drowsy and very calm. He or she has pleasant thoughts and daydreams, and a feeling of well-being and contentment. Also, if the individual has any physical pain caused by illness or injury, the drug dulls the pain.

Some narcotics are medically useful when prescribed by doctors or when they are used properly as nonprescription drugs. Nevertheless, all narcotics can be dangerous because they are addictive. There is a chance of addiction even when narcotics are taken under a doctor's orders. People who abuse narcotics almost always become addicted. Narcotics addiction is one of the most serious drug problems in the United States.

Are Narcotics the Same as Opiates?

An opiate is any drug that is made from the dried sap of the opium poppy. This includes morphine, opium, and codeine, as well as heroin, which is made from morphine.

All opiates are narcotics. But there are also narcotics that are *not* opiates. They are made from various chemicals. Unlike opiates, they are not usually misused or abused. Doctors use them as painkillers and, in the case of methadone, as a treatment of heroin addiction. Methadone will be discussed more fully later in this book. This treatment has been used effectively for years, and recently it has become an important means of helping heroin addicts.

A Short History of Opiates As long ago as 2000 B.C., opium was used by the Egyptians. They collected the white sap from the seedpods of opium-poppy plants and let it harden to form the drug we call opium. They ate small amounts of the hardened sap or made a powder of it to put in drinks. They used the opium to give them a feeling of well-being.

They also tried using it as a medicine for curing many

*(Top) Each pod of these opium poppies growing in Turkey
has been cut to collect the poppy juice. (Bottom) The
dark object is the hardened juice of the poppy; next
to it are two poppy capsules.*

diseases. Although opium did not cure patients, it did reduce their pain and cause them to sleep. Sometimes, if the doses were too strong, the patient died.

In later centuries the use of opium spread to many other countries, including China. But it was not until tobacco smoking spread from Europe to China in the eighteenth century that Chinese opium addicts started to smoke the drug. They smoked the opium in long pipes.

Meanwhile, in Europe and colonial America opium was being used as a medicine. Doctors knew that taking it could be dangerous. But they believed that very small amounts of

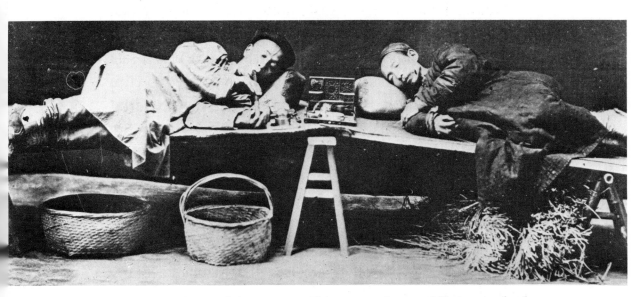

In the eighteenth century, Chinese opium addicts smoked opium in long pipes.

the drug were helpful in treating coughs and other not-too-serious illnesses.

Early in the nineteenth century, scientists began making a powerful new drug from opium. It was called morphine. At first it was taken by mouth. Later, after hypodermic needles were invented, it was given by injection. During the American Civil War, thousands of wounded and sick soldiers received injections of morphine to ease their pain. Doctors soon found that the soldiers became addicted to morphine. Morphine addiction, which became known as the Soldier's Disease, was a serious problem because no one knew how to cure it.

Around 1900 some scientists announced that they had developed a new drug called diacetylmorphine. Although it was made from morphine, the scientists said it was a safe substitute for morphine and could perhaps be used to cure people of addiction to opium and morphine. The new drug was sold under the name heroin.

Heroin did not work as expected. It proved to be much more addictive than any other opiate. In fact, many drug abusers who had developed a tolerance to morphine and opium switched to heroin.

Heroin is now illegal in the United States and most other countries. Unlike the other opiates, it does not have any medical uses.

Morphine is the only strong narcotic drug that is now legal in this country. Doctors still give morphine to patients who are suffering from great pain, but they make sure that the patients do not become addicted to the drug.

Small amounts of opiates are also used in various medicines prescribed by doctors. Certain kinds of cough syrup, for example, have codeine in them. And a medicine called paregoric, which helps stop diarrhea, contains an extract of opium. Although all of these medicines have to be labeled with the warning that they may be habit forming, none of them is dangerous when used as directed.

What Is Heroin?

Heroin is a narcotic drug made from morphine. Most of it is made illegally in Mexico and Southeast and Southwest Asia. It is then smuggled into various countries. In the United States, dealers buy pure heroin and dilute, or cut, it with powdered milk or other substances.

Dealers cut heroin because they can make much more money that way. Also, they know that addicts want cut heroin because the pure drug is so powerful that it can easily kill a person who takes it.

The diluted heroin, which is a white powder, is packaged in small envelopes. Pushers who work for the dealers, and who may be addicts themselves, then sell the drug-filled envelopes to addicts.

Addicts take heroin in one of three ways. They can

Heroin that is being smuggled into the United States is seized by officials of the Drug Enforcement Administration.

"snort" or sniff it. They can dissolve it in a little hot water and then "shoot up," or inject it just under the skin. Or they can "mainline" it by injecting the dissolved drug directly into a vein. Mainlining gives the strongest and quickest effect.

The many different slang names for heroin include junk,

horse, smack, scag, H, and stuff. It is also called dope, but that is a common name for almost any drug.

Why Do People Take Heroin? Heroin is the strongest of all the opiates (it has about seven times the strength of morphine) and it is the most addictive narcotic. Very few people are able to take it occasionally without getting addicted, or hooked. Many addicts start out believing that they can take heroin without becoming addicted. They are sure that addiction "just won't happen to me." But almost always, heroin abuse means heroin addiction.

Then why do people take heroin?

Many young people start taking heroin because they know other people who are already taking it. One student said, "I was at a party, and everybody was having a good time. I wanted to be one of the crowd. I thought if it didn't hurt them, it wouldn't hurt me."

But it did hurt him, for he soon became hooked.

One expert says that when he tells young drug abusers that ninety-eight out of one hundred people who try heroin will become addicts, they answer, "Well, I'll be one of the two who don't."

Why Is Heroin Dangerous? Because heroin is an extremely addictive drug, heroin addicts quickly build up a tolerance to it. Within a few weeks after starting to use it regularly, the addict may need as much as forty times more

heroin than when he or she began. But the person cannot just stop taking the drug, because severe sickness would result. The greater the tolerance the addict has, the worse will be the withdrawal sickness.

The effects of a dose of heroin do not last long for the addict. When heroin is mainlined, the drug acts quickly, giving the addict a strong feeling of warmth and well-being. This is known as a rush. As one addict has described it, "It's that rush for the first minute, when it hits your bloodstream. It's one minute of heaven, that first jolt. Right after, you feel good. In two or three hours you get nervous, wondering where your next fix [dose of the drug] is coming from."

Heroin is expensive. An addict may need hundreds of dollars a *day* to purchase enough heroin to feed a habit. After the effect of the last fix wears off and the addict feels less sleepy, he or she starts trying to find the money to buy more heroin.

It is a race against time. If the addict can't buy more heroin soon enough, he or she will suffer the agonies of withdrawal sickness. That is why so many addicts turn to crime.

Stealing, burglary, mugging, and other crimes are the only way to get enough money. Even if they can get jobs, few addicts can keep them. It is also unlikely that the job will pay enough money to cover the cost of the drug they need.

Addicts break the law in the ways they obtain money and by buying and owning heroin. So they are almost certain to be arrested. This means that if convicted, an addict will have a police record and may have to go through withdrawal sickness in jail.

There is also an additional danger. When addicts buy heroin, they don't know how much the drug has been cut

It is against the law to misuse drugs, but drug abusers also break other laws when they commit crimes to get money to buy illegal drugs. Many of them are arrested, and they often have to face withdrawal sickness in jail.

until after they take it. This means the addict runs the risk of spending money on a white powder that may or may not have heroin in it, that may have been cut with something poisonous instead of milk sugar, or that may have *too much* heroin in it. When there is too much heroin, the addict ODs, or overdoses.

An overdose of heroin can kill a person. The drug induces a very deep sleep and slows the rate of breathing. As a result, too little oxygen is taken into the body, and the user dies.

Addicts suffer from poor health and serious illnesses because they usually don't care about anything except getting and taking heroin. They eat and sleep poorly, which lowers resistance to colds and more serious illnesses. Many addicts don't bother to use a clean needle when they mainline, so that they often get and spread serious infections. When addicts share a needle, they quickly pass the infection from one to another. The frightening increase of acquired immunodeficiency syndrome (AIDS) among addicts is caused by sharing hypodermic needles. There is no known cure for this fatal disease.

Often, even when ill, an addict won't go to a doctor. He or she may be afraid that the addiction will be discovered and that the doctor may report it to the police. An addict truly believes that only one drug can help him or her, and that drug is heroin.

8

Marijuana, PCP, LSD, and Mescaline

Has your mind ever played tricks on you? Have you ever "seen" somebody or something that wasn't there but seemed so real to you that you were positive it *was* there? Have you ever "heard" strange noises or voices that really weren't there either? If you have, you probably had what is called a hallucination. Hallucinations can be pleasant, funny, or frightening. They can be in black and white or in color.

Most people have hallucinations at one time or another, although they do not know when to expect them. Some people, however, have them on purpose. They do so by taking certain drugs called hallucinogens.

The best-known hallucinogens are marijuana, PCP, LSD, peyote, and mescaline.

What Is Marijuana?

No other drug has as many different slang names as marijuana. In the United States, pot is the most common one. However, tea, weed, hay, maryjane, and grass are also used to mean marijuana. Hand-rolled cigarettes made with marijuana are called reefers, sticks, and most often joints.

Marijuana comes from a hemp plant called *Cannabis sativa*. The plant can reach a height of fifteen feet, with a stalk three or four inches thick. The average growth, however, is about three feet high. In general appearance,

Marijuana is hand-rolled into cigarettes called "joints," "sticks," or "reefers."

This drawing of Cannabis sativa *shows the male plant at left and the female plant at right. The leaves of both produce a sticky substance called hashish. The plant's leaves and stems are dried and chopped up together to make marijuana.*

Cannabis sativa resembles a tomato plant. The plant grows wild in many different regions of the world. It is also cultivated in some parts of Asia, Africa, and Central and South America. Many marijuana users prefer pot that is grown in Mexico, but people all across the United States grow it illegally. Because of its climate, California has more illegal marijuana farms than any other state.

The drug is made from the flowers and seed heads of the plant. After they are picked, they are allowed to dry. Dried marijuana ranges in color from grayish green to greenish brown and looks like shredded tobacco.

The resin squeezed from the flowers and seed heads yields hashish, which is five to ten times more powerful than marijuana. Shaped into blocks, the dried hashish may be light brown to nearly black. Its texture varies from crumbly to hard. The most common slang name for hashish is hash.

People take marijuana by eating it, sniffing it (after it has been ground to a powder), or smoking it in marijuana cigarettes. Smoking, the most popular method, provides the quickest and most powerful effect.

A Short History of Marijuana Marijuana, like opium, has been used for thousands of years. The pleasurable effects of the drug were known to the ancient Chinese, who called marijuana "giver of delight," and to the people of India, who called it "soother of grief." They also used the drug to treat people who were suffering from malaria or from constipation and other minor illnesses. Although the drug did not actually cure sick people, it made life less uncomfortable for them. In India, marijuana was also used in religious ceremonies. Indian religious leaders believed that it could "clear the head and stimulate the brain to think."

Eventually marijuana spread to Europe and South America, but it was not very popular. Marijuana reached the

The ancient Chinese called marijuana the "giver of delight" and gave it to people who suffered from malaria, constipation, and other minor illnesses.

United States in the 1920s, but not many Americans started to use it until the 1960s. Today it is probably the most popular drug with pleasure-seeking Americans. One of the main reasons for this is that pot is the cheapest and most easily available drug.

Is Marijuana a Narcotic? American law used to categorize marijuana as a narcotic. That is why many officials classified the drug with heroin and other narcotics. Recently, though, the law has been changed. Although marijuana is still an illegal substance in some states, it is no longer classified as a narcotic.

Marijuana's scientific definition is unchanged, for scientists have long agreed that the drug is not a narcotic. It does not produce the same effects as heroin, morphine, and other opiates. And unlike all the narcotic drugs, it does not cause addiction.

The Effects of Marijuana The effects of marijuana, like those of any drug, depend on how much is used, how often it is used, and on the personality of the person using it.

A marijuana smoker feels the effects within fifteen to thirty minutes after inhaling the drug. The person begins to relax, feels less worried, and is calm and content. He or she feels at peace with the world. If the smoker is alone, he or she may become very drowsy. But if the smoker is with people who are also using the drug, he or she may become cheerful and talkative. Some smokers laugh and giggle a lot and feel very close to other people in the group.

At this stage, the marijuana smoker is high, or "stoned." This usually means that he or she is experiencing very mild hallucinations. Colors look brighter, and music seems to sound clearer and more pleasing. The smoker gets great pleasure from simply running his or her fingers over the surface of a table or carpet or from touching other people. The effects may last for several hours. After they wear off, the smoker feels fine and remembers everything that happened.

We have just described the effects of taking a small amount of marijuana. But some smokers don't get the same effects, and others do but don't like them. As one college student said, "Marijuana was offered to me and I tried it. Oh, yes, I got definite feelings from it, but I didn't enjoy them."

Most people who smoke marijuana just have a joint now and then. They don't smoke it all the time.

However, some people use large amounts of the drug. They may experience frightening hallucinations. They may also find that instead of forgetting their troubles, they are filled with fears and anxieties. But these effects are rare.

The Good and Bad about Marijuana Until recently, there seemed to be no medical use for marijuana.

However, researchers have discovered that if people who suffer from glaucoma smoke marijuana, the drug arrests the progress of this disease of the eye. The drug also decreases the internal pressure on the eyeball, a painful effect of the disease.

An even more widespread medical use for marijuana is with cancer patients who are undergoing chemotherapy. This method of treating cancer involves using strong anticancer drugs. Although these drugs can work against the cancer, they produce unpleasant side effects, especially nausea and vomiting. The side effects can be so bad that some cancer victims stop using the treatments.

The mind-altering chemical in marijuana, tetrahydrocannabinol (THC), helps reduce the nausea and vomiting, and also increases the patient's appetite. Like most drugs, THC can be taken by two methods. The first is by smoking a marijuana cigarette, the method preferred by most scientists. The THC reaches the bloodstream faster and, therefore, begins working sooner than when it is swallowed. Also, if the cancer victim is nauseated, it is difficult to swallow pills without immediately vomiting. The other way, for less nauseated patients, is to swallow pills containing synthetic THC.

In September 1980 the federal government approved a plan that allows cancer victims to receive marijuana pills. In addition, more than thirty states have passed laws allowing the medical use of marijuana.

Those are good uses for marijuana. But what about the bad effects and the dangers?

All over the United States people are confused about what serious problems may result from using marijuana. And there is good reason for everyone's uncertainty.

At this time, no long-range studies have been completed on the dangerous effects of using marijuana. Small teams of medical experts work in various cities, and each team comes up with its own findings. When they release their new information, they suggest that people forget what they have heard before, claiming that "This is the most up-to-date and reliable information there is."

As a result people are wondering what is correct and which "facts" will be declared wrong next year. Is it surprising that people distrust the latest news they hear about marijuana research? The terrible thing is that we may be ignoring important test results, scientific data that could protect marijuana users.

What is needed is one large research team composed of many types of scientists who will be able to work for years to come up with carefully proved conclusions. But there is no money available for experiments on such a wide scale. The main reason is that not enough people feel strongly that there are severe dangers connected with marijuana use.

Today, however, most scientists are very cautious about giving their approval to marijuana use. The following reasons are the cause of the continued concern.

These boys are using a hookah, or "hubble-bubble," to smoke marijuana.

First, the age at which people begin smoking marijuana has dropped drastically in recent years. The number of young people who have been using marijuana before the ninth grade has nearly doubled since the early 1970s. The use of a drug during the formative years may have serious effects on the development of the body.

Another reason for scientists' concern is that the marijuana being smoked by Americans is much more potent, or stronger, than in the past. In 1975 the average marijuana cigarette contained 0.4 percent of the chemical THC. During the early 1980s, the mind-altering drug was ten times as strong. This worries doctors because THC is fat-soluble and can remain in the body for a week or longer after marijuana is smoked.

Marijuana's immediate effects on the brain have been known for years. The drug is intoxicating and interferes with functions such as coordination and other skills needed for driving. There is no doubt that people who smoke marijuana cannot drive safely. Yet users often believe they drive *better* than usual when they are high on the drug. In recent surveys, 60 to 80 percent of marijuana smokers admitted that they sometimes drive while they're high.

The drug can interfere with brain functions in other ways. For example, if the user already has emotional problems, the marijuana may make them worse. A common bad effect is an "acute panic reaction." The user becomes terrified and believes people want to hurt him or her. Approximately 10,000 persons are treated every year in hospital emergency rooms for such marijuana reactions.

If marijuana may be harmful to the brain, what about the lungs? Marijuana smoke contains 150 chemicals besides THC. The effects of some of these substances are not yet known. One, however, is benzopyrene. This is a known cancer-causing agent. There is 70 percent more benzopyrene in marijuana smoke than in the smoke of a tobacco cigarette. Marijuana cigarettes also contain more tar than is present in even "high-tar" cigarettes.

The method of smoking means more of these chemicals get into the lungs of a marijuana smoker than those of a regular cigarette smoker. A marijuana user inhales deeply, holding the smoke in the lungs for as long as possible; a tobacco smoker tends to inhale lightly and exhale quickly. Another problem is that marijuana cigarettes are not filtered. A recent investigation showed that five marijuana cigarettes in a week were more harmful to the lungs than smoking six packs of regular cigarettes in that week.

The heart is also more strongly affected by marijuana smoke than by tobacco smoke. Smoking marijuana may increase the heart rate by as much as 50 percent. If the user is young and healthy, he or she is in no danger. But people who suffer from any heart ailments may be in severe trouble.

Considering all these known and suspected health hazards, people should realize that they are making an important choice when they decide whether to smoke marijuana.

Should Marijuana Be Made Legal? Many people in the United States think so. They say marijuana is a harmless drug, not even proven to be as bad as alcoholic beverages or cigarettes. Other people disagree. They say that marijuana is harmful and that it leads to the use of more powerful drugs.

An argument set forth by marijuana defenders is that if the government watched over marijuana production, the standard of all marijuana cigarettes would be the same. Marijuana smokers face a real problem today. They can never be sure of the illegal marijuana they buy. The marijuana may be weaker or stronger than they expect. Even worse, some marijuana may be laced with dangerous drugs such as PCP, LSD, or even strychnine, which is a poison.

While it is true that governmental regulations would produce a standard marijuana cigarette, would users buy those cigarettes? Evidence has shown that Americans keep seeking marijuana with more and more THC. Marijuana smokers might become dissatisfied with the legal marijuana and once again buy their marijuana on the street.

What about the other laws regulating the growth and use of marijuana? Laws vary from state to state. For example, in some states it is illegal to have even one marijuana plant in your home, whereas in other areas this is permitted. In all states, however, it is illegal to grow large amounts of marijuana.

Certain states, such as California, have made it legal to possess small quantities of marijuana for "personal use." On the other hand, even having a teaspoon of marijuana is strictly against the law in other states. To make matters even more confusing, there are places where marijuana is illegal but the law enforcement agencies don't pursue the users; the police or sheriff's departments feel that there are more serious criminals they must track down.

The only fact everyone can be sure about is that widespread legality is still far off. There is little chance of nationwide legalization until or unless our medical experts become convinced that long-term use of marijuana is safe.

PCP

"PCP [Angel Dust] produces more violent behavior changes [in a user] than any other illegal substance....The public *must* be made aware of the dangers of PCP in no uncertain terms."

Those sentences appeared in a bulletin to all members of the Los Angeles County Sheriff's Department in California.

There is nothing angelic about angel dust. It is truly the devil in disguise. Yet it is still widely abused.

The scientific name is phencyclidine hydrochloride. Most people call it PCP or angel dust. The drug was first made in the late 1950s. In 1963 the Food and Drug Administration (FDA) approved the experimental use of the chemical. The trade name was Sernyl, and it was used as an anesthetic. But researchers discovered that its effects were highly unpredictable. Patients who took the drug often became violent and hallucinated. By 1967 the drug was withdrawn from human consumption.

Between 1967 and 1969 angel dust was being sold as an illegal drug, especially on the West Coast of the United States. However, young people found the results of taking PCP so terrible that they rejected angel dust. By the end of 1969, PCP had practically vanished from the illegal drug market. From the late 1970s until the early 1980s, however, there was a steady rise in the use of angel dust, especially among young teenagers. The average abuser was fourteen years old. One reason for its popularity was that PCP was inexpensive to buy.

PCP is especially dangerous because it is made in home labs. The person who prepares the drug may be a high-school student using some handwritten notes passed on by another person. Two active ingredients are sodium cyanide and hydrochloric acid. If these two chemicals are mixed directly, they produce fumes that are a deadly poison. If even pure pharmaceutical PCP is not safe for humans, then angel dust made by amateurs can only be more harmful.

Whether it is the first time a user takes angel dust or the

one hundredth, the results cannot be predicted. The drug can distort vision, create feelings of excitement, or make the user feel calm and contented. But those effects are not always the ones that occur. Often angel dust causes panic, convulsions, and even paralysis.

PCP users frequently believe they are God or are stronger than God. Because the drug raises the body temperature, users sometimes undress and seek water such as in a public fountain or pool.

Medical help may not be available to a PCP victim. Professionals in hospital emergency rooms are not always able to treat the victim. At times, certain tranquilizers can be given, but too often the doctors and nurses are helpless: Either the victim's body overcomes the drug on its own or death results.

There is an even greater danger connected with angel dust. People who have no intention of using PCP are often tricked into taking it. Many people who buy illegal drugs on the street buy PCP and think it is another drug. Marijuana dealers often secretly dust their marijuana lightly with PCP. They do this because people *can* become physically dependent on the drug. The pushers hope to get new customers for their PCP.

The most common way to use PCP is to sprinkle it over crushed parsley or mint leaves and then smoke it. Angel-dust cigarettes are called hog, mist, and sherman. If a person is given such a cigarette and told it is marijuana, a good test is to smell it before lighting the tip. The odor of parsley or mint will be evident.

PCP can be swallowed, snorted, injected, or smoked. It is available in pills, capsules, crystals, powders, and liquids.

The good news is that in the late 1980s use of angel dust by drug abusers sank to a low level. The bad news is that this happened because users switched to more popular drugs such as cocaine and smack, which are discussed in the next chapter.

LSD

Another drug that continues to rise and fall in popularity among drug users is LSD. The initials are an abbreviation of a long chemical name: D-lysergic acid diethylamide. The slang name for LSD is acid.

The drug is made from chemicals and comes either as a white powder or a clear liquid. Sometimes it is in pill form. Often a tiny amount of the liquid is dropped onto a sugar cube and eaten. Some people even put the drug on the back of postage stamps or envelopes, so they can ingest it by licking. LSD is so strong that even very small amounts of it can have a powerful effect.

The effects of LSD were discovered in 1943 by Dr. Albert

LSD comes in the form of a white powder or a clear liquid. It is most often taken by dropping a tiny amount of the liquid on a sugar cube, which is then eaten.

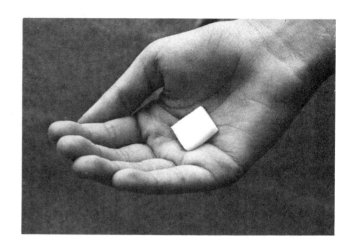

Hoffman, a Swiss scientist. He first took it by accident while he was working in his laboratory. When he became dizzy and restless, he went home to lie down. He began to have strange hallucinations. Patterns of bright color swirled before his eyes. Objects grew and shrank in size. In about two hours, the effects wore off.

Medical researchers experimented with LSD to find ways of curing certain kinds of mental illness and other serious illnesses. There were even cases where people in the United States military services were used as guinea pigs without being told of the drug's effect or its dangers. Today, few scientists see any medical value in LSD. Doctors are not allowed to prescribe it for any patients.

It is a drug that is now made and taken illegally. It is not addictive. But it is so powerful that taking it even once can be disastrous.

Taking a dose of LSD is called tripping. Within thirty minutes the user is on a trip that can last from two to ten hours. It may be a good trip or a bad one. There is no way to predict the outcome.

A good trip may be filled with beautiful sights and sounds. Some people claim they can *see* sounds and *taste* colors while they're on an LSD trip. On a bad trip, a person can have hallucinations that are more frightening than a nightmare. Although nothing the individual sees, hears, or smells is real, the user believes that everything is truly happening.

The LSD user is never sure whether he will have a bad trip or a good trip. This is how a person may look to the LSD user.

LSD's effects are so powerful that they never really leave the body or mind. Days or even months after it is first used, LSD can produce flashbacks, or "return trips." In fact, flashbacks have happened as long as three years after someone has taken LSD. And these trips occur even though no more LSD has been taken.

A person may be walking on the street or sitting in a classroom. Suddenly he or she goes into a dream world, again having hallucinations that may be "good" or "bad." While tripping out, the victim may hurt someone else, but it is more likely that self-injury will occur. LSD users, believing that they could fly, have jumped from ten-story buildings. Some have drowned because they imagined they could walk on water. Some, thinking they were not fit to live, have attempted to kill themselves.

Scientists have not yet found out exactly how LSD affects human beings. Some of them think it seriously damages the brain, nervous system, and other parts of the body. Because no one can be certain about the possible effects, more and more people are saying that they don't want to try LSD even once.

Peyote and Mescaline

Another hallucinogen, with effects similar to those of LSD, is peyote. It has been used for over 150 years by native

Americans of Mexico and the southwestern United States in connection with religious rituals and ceremonies. Peyote is a small, spineless cactus that grows in the Rio Grande region of Mexico and the United States.

Mescaline, a white powder, is obtained from mescal buttons, the tips of the small, round stems of the peyote plant. Although mescaline is not addictive, many scientists believe that its use can cause brain damage.

9

Cocaine, the Not-So-Glamorous Drug

The pro football player charges down the field. Only ten yards separate him from a touchdown. He sidesteps an opponent in black and gold. Five yards. Two. And then he makes it.

He slams the ball to the ground and dances while thousands of fans cheer. All across the United States, people in living rooms and barrooms yell his name, too. Tonight, TV newscasts will show the film of his game-winning play. Tomorrow his photograph will be in every major newspaper. Even while he hops with excitement, he knows the team owners will give him that new contract he wants: three million dollars over the next two years.

If you were that football player, would you give up all that fame and money just so you could get high on a drug?

Too often in newspapers and on television we learn about professional athletes who do just that. But when they took their first dose of the drug, they never imagined the disaster it would bring into their lives.

The drug?

Cocaine.

What Is Cocaine?

Cocaine is a stimulant, which means it speeds up the brain's activity. Although it was once used as a medicine to kill pain, it has little medical use today. But, unfortunately, it is widely misused and abused.

Cocaine comes from the leaves of the South American coca plant, which are made into a white, odorless, fluffy powder. On the street, cocaine is called snow or blow or coke.

In September 1980 the White House released a statement expressing concern over the widening use of cocaine. There was good reason for the message. During the preceding few years, Hollywood directors and performers as well as professional athletes had been arrested for taking cocaine.

Those incidents confirm news reports that more and more people are ignoring the dangers of cocaine abuse in

These women in a South American market are selling the leaves of the coca plant. Later the leaves will be ground into a white, odorless, fluffy powder that addicts either sniff or inject.

seeking a high. Cocaine became the "glamour drug" of the 1980s because of the famous people who have been caught using it.

There are three different ways that abusers of cocaine can take the drug. Many sniff, or snort, cocaine powder. Other people inject the drug directly into a vein. Some mix heroin and cocaine, injecting the combined drugs into the body. This is called a speedball. The cocaine speeds up the action of the heroin.

Why Do People Risk Using Cocaine? What is the high that cocaine abusers desire?

The person may experience a feeling of great happiness. There's an alertness that some people compare to that received when taking another powerful stimulant drug called speed. The abuser feels very strong and bold. Appetite dwindles, and the ability not to feel pain increases.

But the risks of a cocaine high are indeed great. First, because they feel strong and bold, abusers may attempt to do things that they do not really have the strength to do. Physical injury can occur. Large amounts of cocaine may produce a feeling of tremendous fear. The abuser believes that people all around want to hurt him or her. Hallucinations can occur. The respiratory system, or breathing organs, may fail, and the difficulty in breathing may cause death.

For the snorters, long-term use burns the nostrils.

Smuggled cocaine seized by police and customs officials will be destroyed so that it cannot reach users on the street.

73

Sniffing cocaine can even burn holes through the center ridge of the nose, creating a gap connecting both nostrils.

Again, you may ask, why take these risks?

People have been fooled by reports about cocaine. Users tell would-be users, "You can't get hooked on coke."

If they are talking about physical addiction, this is true. Cocaine is not physically addictive. The danger is that users become emotionally dependent on the drug, much more so than they ever imagined they could be. People who abuse cocaine all the time usually seem upset, worried about problems. They also tend to be loners, having few friends. Many cocaine users cannot hold a job because they are undependable workers. Therefore, they lose the means to support an expensive drug habit.

The life of a cocaine user may have some highs, but the lows that may come are not worth the "good" moments.

The Crack Epidemic

During the 1980s a new word entered the drug vocabulary of people in the United States. *Crack*. Perhaps no other drug has received as much publicity, with the exception of marijuana. Unfortunately, while light use of marijuana is probably safe, even light use of crack is dangerous.

The facts are simple. Crack is a more powerful form of

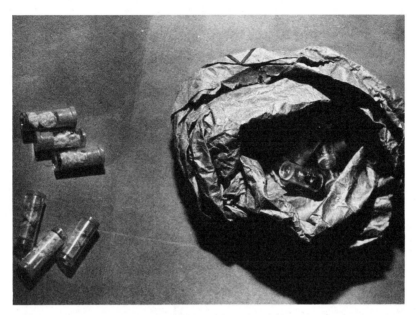

Crack crystals are less expensive than most other illegal drugs—but they are no less dangerous to drug users.

cocaine, a cheaper, smokable form developed in 1986 by drug dealers. Because crack was inexpensive compared to the price of cocaine, sales grew rapidly. Drug users could receive the same effects they got from cocaine but at a much lower price. In 1987 *Time* magazine called crack "the pills with a punch." Crack indeed had punch. But like any misplaced punch, crack could kill—and did.

In 1988 a new type of crack was developed. This kind of crack was called Press or PF (for "Performance"). The aspirin-shaped pill was smoked in a pipe. In addition to the known dangers of this form of cocaine, a new one was added to the list. People who were not drug users found these pills and took them, thinking they were aspirin. Serious illness or death resulted.

Because of the low cost of crack, many new customers

Many people have begun to understand how dangerous crack use is. In New York City a group called the Guardian Angels is helping in the fight against crack.

were now on the street. There was a huge profit in selling crack. At the present time, even small towns across the United States have known "crack houses." These are private homes where cocaine, smuggled in from Central and South America, is converted into crack and sold. A few years ago these small towns were filled with citizens who had trouble believing any of their young people used drugs. Today those same citizens are forced to face the terrible truth.

The high profit of selling crack has attracted vicious criminals. Rival crack gangs murder each other. Often innocent men, women, and children are caught in the crossfire. People who never took an illegal drug in their lives are now dead.

The use of cocaine, whether it's in the original form or sold as crack, is a major drug problem that must be faced by the United States in the 1990s.

10

Depressants, Stimulants, and Other Drugs

Other drugs or substances that are most often abused are model-airplane glue, steroids, barbiturates, tranquilizers, and amphetamines.

Glue Sniffing

Model-airplane glue, or plastic cement, is a special kind of glue that has strong chemicals in it. It is safe when used properly—that is, for cementing models together.

But some people misuse and abuse glue by inhaling, or breathing in, its fumes. They call it sniffing glue. At first the effects are like those of drinking alcohol. The sniffer feels less anxious and more cheerful as he or she starts to get high. But then other effects are felt. The abuser becomes giddy, can't keep his or her balance very well, has trouble speaking clearly, and may vomit. He or she may then become extremely sleepy and finally unconscious. When the glue sniffer wakes about an hour later, he or she usually does not remember anything that happened.

Some glue sniffers never wake up. This is because they sniffed the glue from a glue-soaked cloth that they placed in a plastic bag. Then they put the bag over their head. The bag fit too tightly. They could not breathe after the glue made them unconscious.

Once the abuse of model-airplane glue became known, responsible manufacturers of the products took steps to protect young people. If possible, they removed the high-producing chemicals from the glue. If this could not be done, they added chemicals that would make the abuser sick to his or her stomach.

Some glue sniffers experiment with sniffing the fumes from other products. They may try gasoline, kerosene, shellac, and even nail-polish remover. But few people try it more than once. Each of these substances has chemicals in it that not only can make the sniffer high, they can also quickly make him or her sick.

Steroids

Steroids are drugs that produce two effects that are evident within a few months. The user's body looks more athletic, and muscular development is increased. The dangerous effect is the unseen damage that is done to the liver, heart, and other organs. Death can be the end result of steroid use.

A recent poll of a Tennessee high school showed that 14 percent of the students were taking steroids. Other users include college, professional, and even Olympic athletes. Even more frightening is the fact that some coaches do nothing to stop this harmful practice. Steroid use is obvious to the trained eye. Also, there are tests that reveal the presence of steroids. If the sports leaders do not ban steroids and remove the users from their teams, they are encouraging athletes to harm themselves.

Today, more and more states are making coaches criminally liable if they encourage the use of steroids. Athletes who compete in national contests or the Olympic Games are disqualified for cheating when tests reveal steroids in their bodies.

Unfortunately, many steroid users do not understand that these attempts to ban the harmful drugs are being made to protect them from serious illness or death.

Barbiturates

Doctors call these drugs depressants. Barbiturates depress, or slow down, certain parts of the brain and central nervous system. That is why doctors prescribe them for persons who are suffering from sleeplessness, high blood pressure, or tension.

Drug abusers call them downs or downers. They also refer to them as goofballs or barbs. Today there are over two thousand different kinds of barbiturates. The manufacturers' trade names often end in the letters *al*: for example, Nembutal, Seconal.

A small amount of barbiturates will produce calmness,

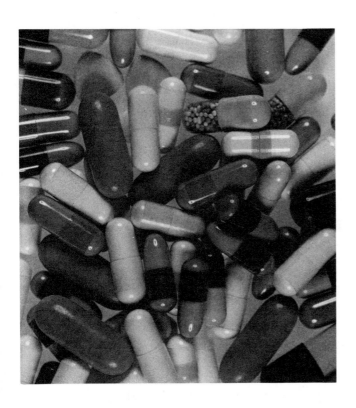

Every year manufacturers produce billions of barbiturates and amphetamines. A lot of them will be used legally by doctors to treat patients. Some, however, will find their way into the hands of drug abusers who have given the pills such nicknames as "red birds" or "blue angels," according to their colors.

relaxation of the muscles, and relief from worry. A larger amount of the drug makes a person stagger and slur his or her speech. If too much of the drug is taken, it has the effect of putting the brain to sleep: the part of the brain that controls the abuser's breathing stops working, and so he or she dies.

Research shows that barbiturates are especially deadly. They confuse a person's mind and mix up his memory. Only a few pills will make someone groggy. The user does not remember how many pills he or she took and swallows some more—sometimes too many. Many people drink alcohol when they have taken barbiturates. The combination is frequently fatal.

One of the worst features of barbiturate abuse is the addiction, or physical dependence, which is high among barbiturate users. Sudden withdrawal from heavy use of barbiturates can cause death.

Tranquilizers

These drugs are also depressants. Although they calm people down, they do not make them sleepy. That is why doctors may prescribe tranquilizers when their patients are especially upset and worried.

There are two types of tranquilizers: major and minor. Major tranquilizers are used in hospitals to treat certain kinds of mental illness. Misuse and abuse of these drugs are rare because the drugs are so difficult to obtain without a doctor's written permission.

Minor tranquilizers are prescribed by doctors for patients suffering from worry and tension. Some minor tranquilizers are Librium, Miltown, and Valium.

Abuse of minor tranquilizers can produce bad side effects. Dizziness, low blood pressure, and fainting are common. Studies suggest that some automobile accidents have been caused by people who took too many tranquilizers.

Tranquilizers can be addictive. Tolerance develops quickly. More and more pills are needed to get that peaceful feeling, so users take more and more. Withdrawal creates vomiting and unhappy feelings.

Other tragedies can happen because of the abuse of tranquilizers. Some of the pills are brightly colored. Babies find the pills and think they are candy. So they eat some of the "candy." Accidental overdoses kill many children every year.

Methaqualone Drugs

On the street, they are known as quaaludes, quads, ludes, sopors, or 714s. On a doctor's prescription, their names will be Quaalude, Sopor, or Mandrax. Whatever the name, these pills contain the drug methaqualone. At one time methaqualone was the sixth most frequently prescribed drug in the United States.

Methaqualone is classified as a nonbarbiturate sedative-hypnotic. A sedative-hypnotic is a drug that can produce two effects, depending on the dosage. A small amount causes drowsiness: the sedative effect. A larger dose will produce sleep: the hypnotic effect.

Scientists had hoped that methaqualone would be a nonaddictive, safe sleeping drug that would replace the more dangerous barbiturates. Unfortunately, the drug is both psychologically and physically addicting. And long-term use builds a physical tolerance to the drug.

The tolerance level is a bit different than with other drugs, especially narcotics. With narcotics, as more and more of the drug is needed to produce the pleasurable effects, the amount that constitutes an overdose usually also rises. This does not occur with methaqualone abuse. The overdose level always remains the same. Soon, as the abuser keeps increasing the dosage, he or she reaches the amount needed to overdose.

The effects that the abuser seeks are similar to those of alcohol. Methaqualone relaxes the user and makes him or her friendly, chatty, and cheerful. But if more of the drug is taken, the abuser feels sleepy, suffers a loss of coordination, and becomes dizzy.

Loss of muscle coordination is also an indication of an overdose, as is slurred speech. The person will have shallow and irregular breathing, experience convulsions, and slip into a coma. The last can lead to death.

As with barbiturates, withdrawal from long-term use of methaqualone can be fatal if it is not done under a doctor's care. Withdrawal sickness produces severe cramps and an illness that is often compared to the flu. The most dangerous part of the withdrawal symptoms are the convulsions, which can be fatal.

Manufacture of methaqualone is now under severe legal restrictions. Therefore, illegal drug sellers cannot obtain large quantities of the real medicine. As a result, the methaqualone that abusers buy on the street may be of two types. The drugs may be manufactured in foreign countries such as England or Canada and smuggled into the United States. But the second variety is more dangerous. Like angel dust and crack, much of the methaqualone sold by dealers is made in home labs. The strength and purity of the drug varies with the person who made the illegal pills. Some do not even contain any methaqualone, but have Valium as a substitute. The amount of Valium is so high that users experience vomiting, cramps, extreme tiredness, and memory loss.

The use of any drug bought on the street is extremely risky. But it is especially true with quads, ludes, sopors,

714s, or whatever name is given to the illegal methaqualone drug.

Amphetamines

Unlike barbiturates and tranquilizers, amphetamines are stimulants: They speed up the brain's activities. At first they were used to treat cold symptoms. People who felt worn out and had aching muscles were pepped up by an amphetamine. Today, doctors prescribe them for weight control (diet pills) or relief of tiredness.

Many amphetamines are sold illegally. Because these drugs stimulate, abusers nicknamed them ups or uppers or pep pills. The most common uppers are Biphetamine, Dexedrine, and Methedrine.

Addicts believe Methedrine is the most dangerous. They call the drug speed. SPEED KILLS is the warning spread throughout the drug world. A "speed freak" takes huge amounts of Methedrine and can become violent without warning. He or she might be talking to you as a friend. Suddenly something makes the person think you are an enemy, and he or she may yell at you or attack you.

When the abuser becomes exhausted, he or she collapses and will sleep for a day or more. Doctors think this drug can damage the brain.

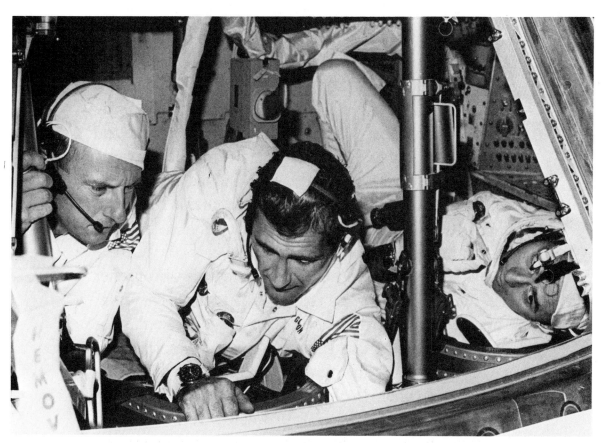

*During space missions, astronauts may use
amphetamines if directed by their doctor, since they must
stay alert in case of danger.*

In the late 1980s a new type of speed called crank was developed. *Newsweek* magazine has labeled crank the "drug of the '90s." And the magazine may well be right.

Crank was first developed on the West Coast. The use of the white, quartz-like crystals spread across the United States like a tidal wave. Designed to be smoked rather than swallowed, crank has many features that appeal to drug users. The new form of speed is cheaper than cocaine, and its effects last longer. The high that crank produces is many times that of heroin. Users also have the feelings of great happiness and peacefulness that LSD can produce. But with crank there is no danger of having hallucinations as there is when using LSD.

The dangers of using crank, however, are also greater than those of other forms of speed. When drug agents enter a house where illegal crank is being made, they must be extremely careful. The agents wear heavy gloves, coveralls, and boots and breathe through a mask attached to an oxygen tank. Otherwise they may suffer harm to their skin, lungs, and liver. If this happens to people who merely touch the raw materials, imagine the harm crank can do when it reaches the interior of the human body.

All amphetamines—not only crank—are dangerous. If the drugs seem attractive because they don't cost much money, users should consider the higher price they may pay.

11

Controlling the Illegal Drug Traffic and Curing Drug Addiction

If we could end drug abuse by passing laws, the problem would have vanished long ago. There are local laws, state laws, federal laws, and even international agreements about drugs.

But the laws themselves are not enough. People have to obey the laws—not only the people who take drugs, but also the people who make, sell, and prescribe drugs.

The Illegal Drug Traffic

The federal government controls the production and sale of drugs in the United States. It tries to make sure that drug companies, doctors, and druggists obey the law. And it has to fight the criminals who make money by manufacturing and selling illegal drugs. This is a very difficult job. Some people say it is impossible.

Amphetamines and barbiturates may be stolen from drug warehouses by dishonest workers. There are also many illegal factories in the United States producing pills for drug abuse. In addition, many home labs are making angel dust, crack, and crank. Large-scale and home laboratories are providing "designer drugs." What does this mean?

Let's say that a substance is declared an illegal drug by the Food and Drug Administration. This usually takes about a year, although the agency can now do it in about three months. Makers of designer drugs then take that illegal drug and change just one minor ingredient in it. That makes the drug different, although only slightly, from the one that has been declared illegal. Now the FDA has to go through the entire process again in order to ban the newly designed drug. Drug manufacturers are always one step ahead of drug officers with their illegal designer drugs.

The problem of smuggled drugs is a tremendous one. Illegal drugs are carried or flown across our borders. They are landed along our thousands of miles of coastline. They are hidden aboard ships and airplanes and carried into our ports. Customs agents at airports and docks and roads check everyone who comes into the United States. Many arrests are made each year. Yet huge amounts of illegal drugs still get into this country.

Specially trained dogs at the Customs Facility in Oakland, California, sniff out packages containing marijuana that have entered the United States illegally.

Crates of legally grown opium which has been pressed into blocks await shipment to companies throughout the world who will use it in preparing legal medicines.

A fishing boat used to bring illegal drugs from South America is seized in Miami, Florida, by the Coast Guard.

Since the late 1960s, elected officials have repeatedly declared war on drugs. These "drug wars" have had little effect. The use of drugs has steadily increased. Organized crime within the United States' borders is heavily involved in the production and sale of illegal drugs. In some foreign countries, government officials themselves help to smuggle drugs into the United States. Illegal drugs are a big business in this and other countries.

But the time may be right to begin winning the war against drugs at last. Until recently the average citizen was not frightened by the drug problem in the United States. People knew about the sale of illegal drugs, but most felt they were not touched by the problem. Now residents in even small towns can look out their windows and see a crack house down the block. Or they hear the gunshots as warring gangs battle.

Perhaps the time has come for victory.

Curing Drug Addiction

Addicts are cured in special treatment centers and in city, state, and federal hospitals. Private hospitals, too, are helping addicts.

In some treatment programs certain drugs are used to help addicts. One of these drugs, methadone, is useful in treating heroin addiction.

Methadone is a synthetic (man-made) nonopiate narcotic. Like heroin, it is addictive, but unlike heroin, tolerance does not develop. This means the methadone addict does not need greater and greater amounts of methadone. It also means he or she can avoid the legal and medical dangers of using heroin. And because methadone costs only a few cents a day, the addict does not have to turn to crime for money.

The methadone programs set up across the United States have been criticized by some people. They say all methadone does is substitute one habit for another. But in the late 1980s there was new appreciation for the benefits of

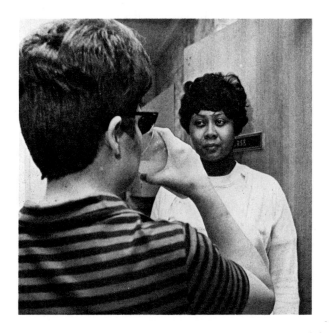

The chief attendant at a treatment center gives a patient her drink of orange juice and methadone. Methadone may only be given by a doctor, a nurse, or other trained specialist.

helping an addict to switch from heroin to methadone. A main cause of the spread of AIDS in the United States is the sharing of needles by drug addicts. If addicts inject methadone at treatment centers instead, they do not share needles and the spread of AIDS is slowed.

Hospitals treating drug addicts face another problem. Babies born to mothers who are drug addicts are themselves addicts. Hospitals call these infants "boarder babies" because they must stay in the hospital for weeks and even months for treatment. In New York City alone, there are 300 boarder babies born *every month*.

In some hospitals, addicts kick the habit by simply stopping their drug taking, a method called cold turkey. Cold turkey can be difficult and even dangerous because of withdrawal sickness.

The cold-turkey method is used in most of the special treatment centers. In these facilities, ex-addicts as well as medical experts treat addicts.

Some of the treatment centers are government-run; others are private. Some are large; some are small. But all of them give hope to addicts who know that they need help in curing their addiction. The names of local centers can be found in the yellow pages of the telephone book under the listing "Drug Abuse and Addiction—Information and Treatment."

There are two great problems in curing drug addiction.

*At Phoenix House, young people who tried using drugs to
solve their problems learn that they can get along
much better without them. Through programs,
re-education, and discussion sessions, they face their
problems to try to find answers.*

First, there are many more addicts than there are places to treat them. Second, if an addict is cured once, the chances are great that he or she will start misusing or abusing drugs again. Why? Because the cured addict returns to the same home and "friends," and because often the reason for the original habit was something in his or her home life or neighborhood or companions. That cause works again on the cured addict, often driving him or her back to drug abuse.

It is much easier to start abusing drugs than to stop. So the best way to avoid drug addiction is to avoid misusing and abusing drugs.

12

Drugs and You

There would be no drug problems if no one misused and abused drugs. Drug pushers would have no customers. Smugglers would make no money. The lives of millions of people would be saved.

How does this problem affect you?

Do you think that you and your friends will ever want to experiment with drugs? You will probably be tempted to try them. You may hear so much about drugs that you will want to see for yourself what they are like. Your friends may try to persuade you to take some. You may think to yourself, "I don't want to be left out. I don't want my friends to think I'm chicken." You may have so many problems at school and at home that you will want to take anything just to feel good again.

But—stop and think again. It takes much more guts to refuse a drug that is offered to you than to accept it.

How can you fight the temptation to use illegal drugs?

Learn as much as possible about your body and your

Young people who were worried about drugs and drug addiction banded together to help themselves and others stay off drugs. At a street fair they passed out information about drugs and asked young people to sign pledges. They called their program "We Can" (We can stay off drugs and help others to do so). They received help from the Youth Services Agency of New York City.

mind. Learn about the chemical substances that can make you sick. You will realize that trying a drug even once may be as dangerous as taking it many times.

Find other ways to learn about yourself. Begin by learning why you do things. Once people understand why they behave as they do, they can better avoid doing something foolish. You will also find that your worries and problems are not unusual. Most of the time we hide the fact that we are scared. We do not want people to laugh at us. But if you have a really good friend, talk about your fears with him or her. That person will most likely admit to having the same ones.

Recently a doctor said, "Growing up is hard. It always has been. But growing up is not something children have to do by themselves. They should be able to get advice from adults."

Which adults can help you?

Not every adult, because not every adult will know you or understand your problems. Remember, adults (in fact, all human beings, young and old) have their problems, prejudices, and fears. Some adults, even the ones closest to you, may not be able to help. But many adults may surprise you by how much they care about you and how understanding they can be.

Pick someone you think will listen to you as well as speak to you. Pick someone you can trust. A young person

If you have a problem, talk to someone about it. Pick someone who knows you and whom you can trust.

who is concerned about drugs usually has several adults to choose from: a parent, a teacher, a doctor, a member of the clergy, a settlement-house worker, a playground director, the parents of friends, or a police officer.

Often just airing and sharing your troubles can ease them and help you to understand them better. Then, even if they don't go away, you can live more easily with them.

In the end, though, you must rely on yourself. Think about what you have learned about drugs in this book and from trusted friends and adults. Think about all you have ahead of you. Remember, you are the only one who can decide about drugs. How you use drugs and whether or not you will misuse and abuse them is up to you.

Glossary

abuse: To seriously misuse drugs for a long period of time

acid: Slang name for LSD

addiction: Being physically dependent on a drug

amphetamines: Drugs that speed up the brain's activities

angel dust: Slang name for phencyclidine hydrochloride

bad trip: Drug-induced hallucinations involving frightening sights and sounds, usually caused by taking LSD

barbiturates: Drugs that slow down the brain's activities

Benzedrine: An amphetamine; slang name, bennies

boarder babies: Babies born addicted to drugs because their mothers are drug addicts

bust: Slang for police raid or arrest

Cannabis sativa: The scientific name for the hemp plant from which marijuana is made

cocaine: A drug made from the coca plant

codeine: An opiate used in cough medicine and as a pain killer

coke: A slang name for cocaine

crack: A more powerful form of cocaine

crank: A smokable form of speed

cut: To dilute a drug by adding another substance

dealer: Someone who buys illegal drugs and often dilutes them for sale to addicts or users

dependence: The state of needing something to lean on for help and support

depressant: A drug that slows down the brain's activities

designer drug: An illegal drug that has been changed slightly so that it is no longer illegal

dope: Slang name for many different drugs

down or downer: Slang name for a depressant or barbiturate

flake: Slang name for cocaine

flashback: Having hallucinations days or even years after taking LSD or similar drugs

glue: Slang name for model-airplane glue or plastic cement

goofball: Slang name for a barbiturate

grass: Slang name for marijuana

H: Slang name for heroin; also called Big H

habituation: A drug abuser's condition of being psychologically dependent on a drug

hallucination: Sights, sounds, and smells that are not real

hallucinogen: A drug that causes hallucinations

hashish: A powerful drug made from the *Cannabis sativa* plant; slang name, hash

heroin: A highly addictive narcotic made from morphine

high: The initial feeling of peace or excitement created by drugs

hooked: Being addicted to a drug

horse: Slang name for heroin

inject: To use a thin, hollow needle to take a drug through a vein or just under the skin

jag: Same as high

joint: A marijuana cigarette

junkie: Heroin addict

kick the habit: Slang term for a drug abuser's giving up the use of drugs

LSD: A hallucinogenic drug; scientific name, D-lysergic acid diethylamide

mainlining: Slang for injecting a drug directly into a vein; also called shooting up

marijuana (or marihuana): The dried leaves and flowers of the hemp plant; also called pot, grass, weed, tea, maryjane, and hay

mescaline: A hallucinogenic drug found in the peyote cactus

methadone: A nonopiate narcotic made from synthetic chemicals

methaqualone: A nonbarbiturate sedative-hypnotic drug; also called quads, ludes, sopors, and 714s

Methedrine: A powerful amphetamine; slang name, speed

mist: A slang name for a cigarette made with parsley or mint leaves and angel dust; also called hog or sherman

morphine: A narcotic drug made from opium

narcotics: Certain addictive drugs that dull pain and cause sleepiness

nonprescription drugs: Drugs that anyone may purchase

opiates: All drugs that come from the opium poppy plant

overdose: An amount of a drug large enough to cause illness or death; to take too much of a drug at one time and therefore become sick or die

PCP: Slang name for phencyclidine hydrochloride (angel dust)

pep pills: Slang name for amphetamines

peyote: A cactus that contains the drug mescaline

popping: Injecting a drug, such as heroin, just under the skin; also called skin-popping

pot: Slang name for marijuana

prescription drugs: Drugs that cannot be bought without a doctor's order

psychedelic drug: A hallucinogenic drug

psychological: Relating to the mind

pusher: Someone who illegally sells drugs for someone else; often also an addict

Quaalude: A trade name as well as a slang name for a methaqualone drug

reefer: A marijuana cigarette

rush: The initial feeling of well-being brought on by use of a drug

side effects: Conditions brought about by a drug that are other than the desired effects

skin-popping: Same as popping

smack: Slang name for heroin

snow: Slang name for cocaine

speed: Popular slang name for Methedrine

speedball: An injectable combination of heroin and cocaine

steroids: Harmful drugs taken to improve athletic appearance or increase muscle development

stick: A marijuana cigarette

stimulant: A drug that speeds up the brain's activities

stoned: Slang name for being high, especially on marijuana

tolerance: The state in which a person must increase the dosage of a drug in order to get the same effect as when he or she began taking it

tranquilizer: A drug that eases worry and tension

trip or tripping: Slang name for when a user takes LSD

turn on: To take drugs

up or upper: Slang name for an amphetamine

Valium: A tranquilizer

withdrawal sickness: Illness caused by an addict's discontinuing the use of drugs

Index

Picture Credits

Abbott Laboratories p. 10

American Cancer Society p. 31

Reggie Blackman p. 98, 100

Walt Boller from *Instructor* © August/September 1970. The Instructor
  Publications, Inc. p. 4

Sue Crooks p. 15, 17

Gil de Varga p. 95

Philippe Giraud/Gamma p. 73

Kenneth Karp/Omni Photo Communications, Inc. p. 27

Ingeborg Lippmann p. 7

NASA p. 87

Nassau County Police Dept. p. 3, 47, 81

Illustration by New York Horticultural Society p. 51

Courtesy Parke, Davis and Company p. 53

Bill Ray—LIFE magazine © Time, Inc. p. 58

Kevin Shaw p. 17, 21, 50, 66

Tannembaum/Sygma p. 44

Allan Tannembaum/Sygma p. 75, 76

Christina Thomson/Woodfin Camp & Associates, Inc. p. 23, 91

Turkish Government p. 40, 67, 91

United Nations p. 40, 72

U.S. Bureau of Customs p. 91

Wyeth Laboratories p. 9

About the Author

Arnold Madison is the author of more than seventy-five short stories and articles, as well as twenty-nine books. Born and educated on Long Island in New York, Mr. Madison worked in education for many years as a classroom teacher and reading coordinator. He now teaches at writers' conferences and speaks at schools and clubs all over the United States. Mr. Madison lives in Amsterdam, New York.